# All Things Painful

Dax Christopher

# All Things Painful
## 3rd Edition

Copyright © 2013 by Dax Christopher

Cover illustration by Schilling Concepts

ISBN 978-0-9889873-3-3

Please visit the author's website
www.daxchristopherbooks.com
for other works and contact information

# Sunrise

# Sunset

*This book is dedicated to you.*

# INTRODUCTION
(A Word of Comfort)

I'd like to tell you that no one will ever let you down, but somewhere along the line someone will. I'd like to tell you that justice will be served, but it probably won't be. I wish I could tell you that she's thinking about you, but she probably isn't. I wish I could tell you that you're all he needs, but you probably aren't. I'd love to assure you that you're not alone, but I can't. I'd like to say that there are no reasons to fear, but there are plenty. I hope that the answers you seek are easy to find, but they probably won't be. I wish I could say that romantic love is worth dying for, but it isn't. I'd like to promise that good news is right around the corner, but it might not be. I wish I could guarantee that the sun will rise tomorrow, but it may not. All I can tell you for sure is that whatever happens—no matter how cold it might get, no matter how lost you might feel, no matter how badly it might hurt—*you will be better for it.* It can't last forever, and I will be here for you until the cessation of all things painful.

## ROSES AND CHERRY BLOSSOMS

There's a garden outside that blooms for no cause,
And as I walk past I have reason to pause.
There's a very light rain and its colors are glistening,
Fragrances dance in the air and I listen
To the sound of the cycles of blossoms and roses;
The sound of the silence that opens and closes
The door of existence, and what do I hear
But the sound of two flowers, both drawing me near.
A soft, subtle tear at a rose petal's death
And the falling of blossoms that gave their last breath.
*You're buried out here, your last place of rest;*
*This is the place where you passed your last test.*
*I forgot you were mortal and mourned you in jest;*
*Now I remember that no one's so blessed.*

There's a tired old rose still hanging on tight
To the stem that has held it so long in the light.
Its petals are dry and they crack in the breeze,
And gone are the days when it lived just to please
All the eyes that beheld it and here it still stands,
Determined to live every minute it can.
Long ago it was lovely, a deep ruby red,
But its delicate looks only hung by a thread.
A tired old rose now well past its prime,
Defiant of laws that have governed its time.

1

*So like a rose to insist that we stay*
*And cling to our petals at the end of the day,*
*Or until the gale forces have torn them away—*
*This is the sound of your life gone astray.*


A cherry blossom falls from its place on the tree,
Bidding farewell to the world it can see.
Accepting the fall at the height of its beauty,
The blossom concedes it fulfilled its life's duty.
No grasping, no struggle, no search for protection
From natural process, no wish for exemption—
For whose life is death not always a part of?
Whose death can life not claim it's the start of?
A fallen young blossom at the peak of its prime,
Seeing no reason to ask for more time.
*To say without saying, to live as though dead,*
*To not need the answers before they've been said,*
*To know what the rules are before they've been read,*
*This is the sound of that life you have led.*


Petty, the practice of dealing for hours;
The garden still grows without two certain flowers.
People still leave and life is still fleeting;
None here among us can forestall the meeting
That's coming as surely as you left us all—
May your journey be safe and your obstacles small.
We roses will miss you; it just seemed too early
For someone like you to be taken, but surely
The first thing you'd want is the last thing you earned—
For roses to give you the rest you deserve.
*When you find your way down from the tree to the ground,*
*Take comfort in all of the blossoms around.*
*A blossom that falls is a blossom that found*
*Its own place in the picture, and this is the sound.*

# THE GHOST OF JOHNNY MOSS

Looking for a game on a Saturday night in Sin City,
where there's no telling wrong from right,
I moved forward through the races, and all the blank
faces, oblivious to the cases of life and love lost.
Tired of the same old song and dance, tired of catering
to Baby's next chance,
Another lesson for me about how life should be and
how I'll never see what love truly costs.
The street was still wet underfoot from the rain, and the
steam rising up carried with it the pain
Of the unwise men who stayed in with two tens hoping
God would soon send some luck and went broke.
I wasn't in the mood to think about love, and had never
expected any help from above,
Just my mind and my game, no friendship, no fame,
with no-limit stakes that I'd claim or I'd choke.

Sitting on the corner of 6$^{th}$ and Mercy Street is a bar
where the sharks and the flounders like to meet.
Each time I've been bitten IOUs have been written and
the numbers forgiven don't add up to much.
It's a place where a guy needs to watch where he's
walking and the men with the guts let the chips do the
talking.
You have to think fast or else you won't last, but in the
past Johnny always came through in the clutch.

My eyes swept the room at the end of my ascension up
the stairs; one table seemed to catch my attention.
Two men there were toking on long pipes and joking
that their game was smoking all others who played.
I went to their corner and threw down my chips, sorted
my stacks, threw the dealer a tip
And said, "I'm a new face in this God-awful place and
if you have the space we'll get underway."

The man with the silver pipe looked amused, while the
one with the gold looked a little confused.
"This game's not for boys, we don't play for toys," one
said, "We'll enjoy watching you as you lose."
"I don't often fail," I said with the air of a man who
thought that the game would be fair.
"Very well, even so, you may want to know who you're
playing even though it's too late to refuse."
"Be who you are," I replied with the same cocky tone
that had gotten me into this game,
"Names don't matter to me, I'd rather you just cut the
chatter and let the game roll."
"I am the Devil, the Divinely Abhorred, and the chap
to your right is my good friend, the Lord.
Since you're so bold to sit here and scold us on talent,
we'll play for control of your soul."

My face lost its color and I broke a cold sweat; this
wasn't a match I had practiced for yet.
My mind set about looking for a way out while I tried
to seem stout and unafraid of this pair.
"Don't bother to leave," said the Lord, "we win if you
can't take the heat and man up to your sin."
As the clock started ticking, my pulse started kicking
my eyes into switching between the two stares.

The prospect of playing was no longer fun, I was telling
myself to turn quickly and run,
But there in my head was a master, long dead, his voice
every shred of old age and tough wins.
He told me to see it all through to The End; have some
faith in the river and a lucky Ace-Ten.
No running away, no choice but to stay, no choice but
to pray and man up for my sins.

Johnny said, "You *are* as good as you've said, but these
two here are out for your head.
No, you're not prepared, but still, don't be scared; your
confidence, repaired, can do more than you'd bet.
Life doesn't always wait 'till we're ready, so when the
chips fall can we make sure we're steady?
You can't come unhinged when there's one chance to
live, and the more you can give the more you can get.
You worry yourself 'cause you know who they are and
they're famous for cheating, but wait 'till the cards
Are dealt to bow out and leave here without any chips;
you're out before the game even starts!
Don't run from your sins or the challenge, just play
with your best face on and make those two pay.
You talked, now improve to the point that you move
Hell and Heaven just to prove that you have the heart."

"I'll need five of those," I said to the air as I sat and
ignored their insidious stares.
"Then we're on," said the Devil as the cards were
disheveled and my gaze turned and leveled on the girl
dealing out.
She looked to be almost exactly my age and I had a
strong feeling that on some other stage

Her blood red eyes would make me realize I should
quickly recognize who she was with no doubt...
But now for the game, it was time for control; I'd be
damned if I'd let them leave with my soul.
The cards were then fanned with the Devil's cut
planned; my heart was a sandbag dead in my chest.
With the Devil on the buck, I had the big blind and
placed it while trying to calm down my mind.
The cards began flying from the vixen and dying right
before me; I was trying to ignore all the rest.

A King-Jack off suit is what I was dealt; it was hard to
control the excitement I felt.
They both called the blind and I raised right behind
hoping three of my kind would fall on the flop.
The Lord and the Devil both saw my strong bet, and I
wondered what hands they had happened to get
Up until the cards fell because then I could tell I would
do pretty well; a King, Three, Jack had dropped.
I fired at the pot like a god had possessed me hoping
each would have faith in his hand and contest me.
The Devil first stalled, then hastily called, but the Lord
looked appalled and turned in his low pair.
The chips were pushed in, and an Eight on the turn
couldn't help him, so feeling I had chips to burn
Another strong bet with zero regret I presented yet
Satan was far from despair.

He called my bets round after unholy round, but with
top two pair I was still safe and sound.
On the river a Six came out in the mix and I knew that
I'd rip Satan off of those chips.
I threw in the money 'cause he didn't have a hand, and
when he called me out I just couldn't understand.

Imagine my shock when I saw that my stock of chips
had been rocked by unlucky trips!
His Sixes face down must've been a cruel trick; my
heart simply sank and my stomach felt sick.
He said, "Tough beat," with a smile so sweet that I
wanted to deck the guy right then and there.
No good player would have stayed in that hand, just
waiting for one lucky low card to land.
And there, as I fought with my anger, one thought in
my head had me caught and I whined, "That's not fair!"

And Johnny said, "Maybe it is, and maybe not; it was
just dumb luck that won him that pot.
Sometimes we make strong moves and we take a good
beating for the sake of others less skilled.
Sometimes we lose, even with a good hand, but the loss
is for nothing if you can't understand
Even though life plays in some shady-like ways you
have to re-raise and remain strong-willed.
True, there's no way he should call your two pair, but
when life calls you out, son, be damn prepared.
Maybe he cheated and should be unseated, or maybe he
needed a card and it fell,
Maybe the dealer *is* out for your blood, and maybe cold
cards *will* be coming in floods,
But know the right course, and don't try to force in a
loss when, of course, it's too early to tell."

Our dealer got up, just the first of three fated, which
was fine by me since I thought her deals tainted.
She flashed a quick grin at me then motioned in her
replacement, a thin, lovely girl with grey eyes.
At once I felt certain I had seen her as well, but alas, it
all faded before I could tell...

She sat down to deal; I just had to feel that none of it was real except in my mind.

Misguided, of course, I was there just the same with a shortening stack and a frustrating game.

And of course, I was nervous, as this dealer's service was likely on curve with the one who just left.

The two at the felt table with me were fervently playing for rights to my soul, and concurrently

I was quite shaken, my stacks would be taken unless I awakened and ceased all their theft.

The cut of the deck was left up to God, with a tip of his hat and a slight, cordial nod.

Out came the cards, such ominous shards that were playing the guards of my soul on that night.

I looked with dismay after posting my blind at the Ten-Four suited that put me behind

My two tough opponents; I had the components to lose, so that moment I had to play tight.

The Lord opened up with a deified raise like the hand he had pulled had been waited on for days.

The Devil, almost knowing just where the Lord was going, called it, all but showing both of us the hand he got.

The price to keep playing was a little too rich; I had two clubs it was nuts not to pitch.

The thought made me frown, but I couldn't play around with low numbers down whether suited or not.

The flop came Ten, Ten, Four, center stage—it was all I could do to push back all my rage.

I sat there without my winning full house and tried not to pout so the others could see.

The hand was played on, but I stared at the felt, simply livid that I folded the hand I was dealt.
Nearing wits' end, in a room with no friends, I would have to make amends with a win that wouldn't be.
Still cursing myself for a stupid decision, I felt a strong need for a brief intermission.
I no longer cared if a chip and a chair was how well I fared after this kind of game.
Not knowing what I could possibly do, I leaned way back for a second or two
And almost gave up; I'd had about enough of this "unlucky" stuff when foul play was to blame.

And Johnny said, "You haven't made a bad call, there was no way to know those cards were to fall.
Because you get burned ain't a reason to turn in or hang up your spurs; you still have a stack!
Because something seems to work out in your favor still ain't half a reason to sit back and savor
That call as a winner; you're still just a sinner who fell for luck's glimmer—now get it all back!
Don't let luck make you think that your moves are all wrong just because you've done nothing but lose.
The flop, turn, and river can make us all shiver but they can't give or take from us all the right plays.
Don't look twice at a hand that you've folded; at cards or in life the events that you've molded
You can't be regretting, 'cause then you start letting your loss be the setting and drive in your ways."

The Lord won the hand I hadn't bothered to watch with a Queen-high straight, just one narrow notch
Over Satan's Jack-high, earning one snide reply, after others too dry, that was safe to repeat.

Short stack or not, I was freshly inspired by the words
Johnny Moss counted quickly and fired
Like the chips he had played during his glory days that
had come through and made more wins than bad beats.
Come Hell or Heaven I'd stand and deliver with the
cards I was dealt standing in as care givers.
So back in the game, no friendship, no fame, I had
Johnny's name ringing clear in my head.
The stacks made it look as if I was in trouble; I was low
man, so I'd try hard to double.
I could play tight, but I thought that I might catch them
sleeping if I tried out some loose play instead.

Then the Lord spoke up, "Your predicament's grim; in
two hands we've made those stacks of yours slim."
Said the Devil, "I confess, I feel rather blessed now that
our contest seems to lean my way."
I said, "Just put out your blinds and repent, I'll no
longer count on luck being sent."
I threw both a stare, then pulled in my chair, took in the
air and said, "No more to say."
The silver-eyed dealer got up from her seat; it was time
for a new face to deal out the heat.
Out came a guy, complete with a tie and a visor,
stretched too wide and low to see features.
I felt a bit safer; there wasn't that plight of swearing I
had seen him before that night.
I was wondering still, underneath the green bill, what
color was filling the eyes of this creature…

My questions could wait for the next rainy day; focus
was needed if I would get paid.
I kept a stern frown as I looked at my down cards
although luck had found me a mighty Ace-Ten.

The rest of my life seemed so far away as I put my
soul's fortune on both of those spades.
No thoughts of romance or Baby's next chance or
friends or finance—it was all erased then.
In the cosmic importance of the moment I vowed to
never again get lost in the crowded
Feelings which let me become upset with events that
had never lent room for control.
Life was a game to be played with some focus, with no
time for thoughts and feelings that soak us
In our own self doubt, and our own self clouding of
judgment without first searching our souls.

I called the big blind and raised only a bit; I didn't want
the Lord or the Devil to quit.
They both seemed happy and called in the snappy
manner of two trappy amateurs on the strip.
When the flop came out I took nothing for granted, but
it couldn't get better even if I had planned it.
Out came my Aces, by the dealer's good graces, so then
I hoped faces would give them both trips.
Ace of Clubs, Nine of Clubs, Ace of Hearts fell, the
Lord checked to Satan, not giving any tells.
The Devil bet small, most likely on a draw for a flush,
or he already had a low pair.
My Aces just had to be played to the max; I couldn't
just let them stand over their stacks
And let free cards fall since they were on draws that
could beat my three Aces when all's fair and square.

I pushed in a bet that would make them both shrink,
but they beat me in the pot without having to think
About what I might've had, I thought their play radical
and not a little sad; I had the best hand.

The dealer took the top card off for the burn, and the
Eight of Diamonds made itself known on the turn.
The Lord again checked, and the Devil, perplexed by
my raise last round, pecked the table with his hand.
I bet strong again, very sure that my Aces could send
them both packing to their native places.
They both had to think; Satan ordered a drink and God
had to sink down low in his chair.
Maybe because they were running so hot it just didn't
matter if they drew well or not.
They crowded the center, each trying to measure my
hand; it was better for me not to stare.

Waiting for the river I felt time freeze; I knew that card
could bring us all to our knees.
In the moment of Zen, out came the Ten of Clubs on
the end of the board we were watching.
That filled me up, I was in the top slot, and I knew that
I would be walking home with that pot.
But I still had a chance to reel in and dance with these
two and prance off with the win they'd been notching.
I could have all their chips if I faked the right tells
before either bet so they'd think all was well.
I sent up a prayer when the Ten fell, a layer of sorrow
and wishes for my savior to come.
A prayer that no one would call out my bluff, that I
tried to hold on but never got the right stuff.
God heard the cry and went all-in to try and take what
was left of my broken down sum.

I knew that the Devil had his eyes on me closely, so I
kept mine down and spoke to the felt mostly.
I muttered a curse in a preconceived verse that luck
should've reversed and given me a due break.

Satan had keyed on the angst I was sending and went
all-in behind God, not pretending
To hide what he had, thinking my hand was bad and
preparing to grab what he wanted to take.
Somehow I knew God pulled out his straight, and Satan
had his flush so they both took the bait.
I took a breath in, manned up to my sins, pushed my
chips in and said, "What are you holding?"
They both stopped and stared at me, clearly surprised
that I called, and too late did they come to realize
That I had them both beat; when they did, there was
heat coming off of those seats—they regretted not
folding.

Full house, Aces over Tens beat the flush and the
straight that I knew they would play and I'd crush.
I took all the money they had in the stunning wake of
all the running cards we had just seen.
Their shock and dismay are a treasure I've kept every
night since then as I've laid down and slept.
They rose with disgust at their "unlucky" bust and I
was entrusted with my soul and my dreams.
"When are you boys gonna realize the truth, that you
shouldn't claim souls without any proof
Of what's right and wrong, or where justice belongs, or
who sings the songs that put all in good graces?"
I kept on, "Maybe you shouldn't use cheating to get the
support you think that you're needing.
And if you both think I'm just here to sink your teeth
into and drink—tell that to these Aces."

They both left the table and the room without words
and got lost in the night, altogether unconcerned.

They never looked back to see all their stacks being put in my rack—it was better that way.
The dealer looked up with a kind, gentle smile, "I expect they'll remember that hand for awhile.
Well done, sir, well read, well played, and well said, you shredded their egos, son, that I must say."
I said, "Thanks pal, have a few of these chips," as I slid over to him the mother of all tips.
He said, "Thank *you*," with a smile so true it could take all the blue off a guy feeling down.
"I always hate seeing those two win, each trying to peddle some virtue or sin.
The downside there is real players play fair, and we wouldn't ever dare to cheat life for a crown."

"Don't worry about Baby, or anything else," he said, "you'll be fine if you just be yourself.
You got a good start, and an even better heart, and I think that your part in life will soon show."
He nodded and stood and made way for the door—no, I had never seen that guy before...
As I turned back around to the table, I found that his visor had dropped to the ground, and some flow
Of suspicion had crept its way into my mind—why would he leave his green visor behind?
I looked back, aghast at exactly how fast the Grand Old Man had blasted away, and I felt
A swift, sudden need for a thorough review of the night and the dealers that we had gone through.
And so I searched swiftly for a story that fit me and right then it hit me just what I'd been dealt...

## KAISHAKU, PART I
(Farewell to No One)


Dim the lights and stall tomorrow,
Curb your worry, end your sorrow.
One more night with you is all I have,
so make it last.

Let the past be what it may,
Take the future day by day,
We can't help we never met,
The End just came too fast.

Now I know that you were there
Hoping I'd show up somewhere,
But knowing just like me our paths
were never meant to cross.

So even though our feelings burned,
Year by year we slowly learned
Just as our love was never found,
it also can't be lost.

*So kiss the sun goodbye, my love,*
*It's now my time to die, my love,*
*We're both too strong to cry, my love,*
*That river's long been dry.*

All our lives we've done our best,
Not once needing pause for rest,
Never kneeling, never bowing down
when life got tough.

What we had to give, we gave,
Knowing we might find the grave,
And through it all, we found that what we gave
was not enough.

We never turned our eyes in shame,
No reassurance ever came
That we would beat the world at all the
petty games it played.

And still it never broke us down,
And other's tears could never drown
The light we had, and all our time
was spent so unafraid.

*So hold your head up high, my love,*
*Life didn't pass us by, my love,*
*It's futile asking why, my love,*
*We know how hard we tried.*

Life was hard, but so were we,
While never sure of what to be,
Strong until the bitter end,
defying life's visage.

Trusting no one more than fate,
Never giving in to hate,
Although it was unfair our hope
was only a mirage.

And at The End, I've been impressed
By how you withstood every test,
And time and time again you came through
smile all aglow.

So carry on without regret,
Your story's still not over yet,
And know that Hell won't matter to me
if that's where you go.

*I know it isn't fair, my love,*
*But this I'll always swear, my love:*
*For you I'll always care, my love,*
*If only time was there.*

## KAISHAKU, PART II
### (No Place for a Warrior)


The sun is setting on my weakness tonight.
The past and the future are both out of sight.
Gone are the laws pushing wrong against right,
Dust in the wind with a fool's wish to fight.

The way has been long; my weapons are heavy,
But here, at The End, next to you, I stand ready.
I pray that my mind and my hand remain steady
For my strength wants to fade with my honor already.

My effort was there, my intentions were clear,
Still clueless toward which of life's paths I should steer.
But one single thought I could constantly hear
Singing *"There is no place for a warrior here."*

There is no time left for searching your soul,
There is no patience for strong self control,
No one here thinks they should pay the last toll
For the life and the spirit our existences stole.

Love is a feeling found only in dreams
And people are rarely just as they all seem.
And through all the glitter and marketing schemes
All I can hear is a malcontent scream.

So there is no place for a warrior here.
I won't see The End as a time to be feared.
I won't waste the moment by shedding my tears
Over times that are lost in the haze of past years.

So there is no urge to refrain and ask why,
I already told my lost Love not to cry.
I was built for The End, my Love can't deny
That when all's said and done it's a good day to die.

In a world full of weakness I always stayed strong,
And I meant to do right even when I was wrong.
I wouldn't stop fighting when fights would run long,
And all at the cost of somewhere to belong.

You won't see fear in my eyes anymore,
You won't find a mind that exists to keep score.
My primal side emits one continuous roar
As I stare down the world that never bothered before.

In a moment of weakness, though, I lost my mind
At a time when my selfishness made my heart blind.
I lost my capacity to help and be kind;
For an hour I left my compassion behind.

So somewhere I gave under just enough strife,
And for that infraction I forfeit my life.
I pray that my nerves can help steady this knife
As I fall to my knees and I forfeit this life.

Because there is no place for a warrior now,
In a world where you're heard as long as you're loud,
In a world where you're no one apart from a crowd,
My thoughts and my feelings simply won't be allowed.

So don't cry for me, rest easy my friend.
It's a lie to suggest I don't welcome The End.
After life, Hell and Heaven can't hope to contend
With all I lay down just to find peace again.

# FORMLESS LIKE WATER

Take this gently, now.
Just a soft trickle of a reminder, a nice piece of friendly
advice, if you like.
Or, a desperate plea, if you like that better.
I suppose it goes that it depends on how much
attention you pay to your own well being.
I don't wish to be forward, so let's start quietly.
Now, with the days getting long, I can feel something
wrong at my outer limits;
A slow, dull, nagging, unsettling pull.
You've paid more attention to your rockets, rings, and
other pretty things than you have to me.
I don't blame you; I can be easy to forget.
You use me, change me, dress me up, derange my
chemical makeup to suit your tastes.
I allow it because resistance goes against my nature.
But taking me for granted is a mistake too heavy-
handed even for you.
Like it or not, you need me to survive.
I'm everywhere--around you, above you, below you, in
you--but without a form to call my own.
But that doesn't mean I'm not alive.
*I am formless like soul, and I'll play my own part*
*Just as surely as tides track the beat of my heart.*
*I can weave like a story through all that I see;*
*I am formless like soul, and it is formless like me.*

Let me help you remember.

Think of your fondest memories, those summer evenings when the sun is bronze and your hair is just a touch blonder from exposure to the day's rays.

Take me out of a single frame, and the entire movie changes.

The lemonade turns to powder and you cry just a little louder for shade, and your flowers are wilted because your garden hose just coughs up dirt.

My fluidity, my influence, my magic, are gone.

Take me out of a single frame, and your entire world turns to grey; there's absolutely no shame in admitting this and there's no point in blaming me for it.

Your animosity wouldn't change the facts.

Remember when you wanted to be healthier? You made me an even bigger part of your life, and everyone else said it was too much work, but not me.

It was obvious that you couldn't do it without me.

I've been there to help cure what ailed you, helped you clean up your life when other methods failed you, I've never asked a favor or tried to derail you.

Because we're not so different, you and I.

Trying to get by in the same world, swirling in and around ourselves aimlessly until we find the path of least resistance.

Fate delivered us to each other, for better or worse.

*I am formless like love, and I pour from your eyes,*
*And I'm there every day as you cry those eyes dry.*
*I can comfort you, warm you, and do it for free;*
*I am formless like love, and it is formless like me.*

Show some respect.

Generations of warriors have lived and died trying to

emulate a way of life that comes naturally to me, yet you take my effort so lightly.
I don't pretend to be perfect.
I know I have a furious temper, but I'm calm at my center and try to remember that it isn't necessarily all bad.
Some things in this world need to be broken.
And I don't regret my ferocity, because that's what gets all your big plans to come to fruition, and makes the world check itself when it matters.
It's good to remind people you're not a doormat.
Give me enough time and I'll move mountains for you; learn how to ask and I'll create fountains for you; I've trusted you not to overstep your bounds.
But some things need to be said more than once.
I never intended to cause trouble; I have no intention at all, but your face keeps invading my space like there's no other place in the world it could be.
Are your sand castles really that important?
*I am formless like strength, I was here long before*
*The great wheels of your mind had begun to keep score.*
*I can crash with a hurricane's force on the sea;*
*I am formless like strength, and it is formless like me.*

Give me the chance.
Give me the chance to show you what I can do when you treat me as an equal and together we can write a sequel, instead of a finale.
It takes a collective effort to make it better.
But once we do, I can wash away pain, our new domain will be this brave new plane and we can put a little more sane back into this world gone crazy.
So what do you say?
You've never given me a sign that you're paying any

attention, but my contention is that eventually the
reality will be too urgent for you to ignore.
Because like I said before, we both know you can't live
without me.
Stay prideful if you must, but I trust that over time the
rust will get rinsed out of that hustling mind of yours,
too busy to see the long term.
And on that day, I'll be waiting.
I'll be waiting, in season or out, good reasons or bad,
pleased to see me or not, teased about coming back,
and together we'll ease back into the natural order.
On that day, I'll be waiting.
*I am formless like hope, I can right all the wrongs,*
*We can make this a world where you want to belong.*
*People say it's too late, but I'll never concede;*
*I am formless like hope, and it is formless like me.*

# NEGATIVA

Envy knows her precious mind and doesn't care if she's
unkind,
Hiding razors in her words with looks that make you
blind.

Envy takes the easy way and lets you fall so she can say
She would've been there had you only listened
yesterday.

Envy's always on the move 'cause Envy always has to
prove
To people who she's burned her life will sure enough
improve.

Friends she makes end up in nets of foolish hopes and
false regrets,
But she's alright as long as she can keep all that she
gets.

Up and down, get down and look at what you found,
she wrote the book
On what you lost; that moment you were out was all it
took.

Introductions come and go, all move fast but you're too
slow,

The details of her life are simply not for you to know.

Left and right, what's right or wrong just have no place in Envy's song;
As long as you have faith in what she does then you'll belong.

When she turns and shows her back, you don't know if she'll attack—
It all depends on where and how and why the chips are stacked.

*So have your guard up when the Diva, standing in her negativa,*
*Looks your way and waves you over just to have a chat.*
*Be careful when her back is turned, and never touch or you'll get burned,*
*You never know just when she blows up, crazy like a cat.*

Envy's words are always true as long as they don't hinder you,
But what you think is green, she says, is only seen as blue.

Envy walks a tight, high wire, masking hatred with desire,
Always moving fast enough to stay smooth under fire.

She needs love and cries to get it; she needs cash and tries to spend it;
Every chance you give her, man, you're sure to soon regret it.

Always fun to satisfy, Envy lives a constant lie,

But you're her one and only, man, so hey, give love a try.

Your broken heart she'll sell for cash and add it to her private stash,
And disappear one day just so the two of you won't clash.

Families that take her in all fall apart because her sins
Are turned into a game that all will play but none can win.

People always take the bait because they all appreciate
The kind of life she's had and feel so sorry for her state.

But women scorn and husbands cheat, money walks on Envy's feet,
And out the door she goes, her hips a jinga down the street.

*So now they all look for the Diva, always with that negativa,*
*Angry and dejected since they've all been burned and used.*
*But Envy never lets her eyes meet yours for if you see her lies*
*Then every time you fight with her she's always doomed to lose.*

*Because the girl may never see a liar never stays at ease*
*She'll spend her years just running every time she gets found out.*
*Honesty may never seem to Envy like a valid scheme,*
*And so it goes that lovely pose will always be without.*

# THE MARCH

When shells are exploding and mayhem's unfolding,
When everyone runs and you and I are left holding
In one hand the prize and in the other the lies
That they thought would all help us, we never will hide.

They told us we shouldn't and told us we couldn't,
And now they're all fools for believing we wouldn't
Stick close when it mattered—now *they* split and scatter
And here we are, both still climbing that ladder.

We wrecked both our cages and marched through the
ages,
Soldiers in a war that this society wages
With misunderstanding and stern reprimanding;
Now we're the only troops half worth commanding.

We've fought in the trenches, we've come off the
benches
And won the games no matter how many wrenches
They tried to throw in; we still got the wins
And threw them right back in their sly, hateful grins.

You're the best man I know, you've seen how we've
grown
And now I'm at your service anywhere you might go.
We'll keep marching on, though the daylight is gone,

y steel drum guides our steps toward the

If your world turns around, if what's up becomes down,
I'll be the first one to plant your feet on the ground.
When a cold day in Hell will come, no one can tell,
But I'll push it all backwards to find where you fell.

Keep marching, my friend, for this war will never end,
It's just you and me making all the rules bend.
When the firefights come, I'll still hear that drum,
And I'll take the first bullet shot out of the gun.

I would lay it all down, 'cause that's what you deserve,
I would take every bullet and steel all my nerves.
I would give it all up in the blink of an eye;
At the end, my best man, I would lay down and die.

# ANOTHER DEAD CORSAGE

The moon sheds light on my mood and our tragedy
Better than the sun ever did.
We're long overdue for that walk we put off
And the compromising we never did.
It only rains during the nighttime here
And the summer sun burns in my brain.
I've been standing here, waiting here, patiently looking
For a sign that never once came.

And now I feel my love is freezing,
Clutching for the air that's leaving;
While the sunset warms and lights it,
Everything within me fights it.
I don't want that second chance
They never gave me—or the dance
That tact and basic impulse promised;
They saw no point in being honest.

*It's just another life that I can't be a part of...*
*It's just another dream that I'm not allowed to share...*
*It's just another dead corsage for me to burn into my memory;*
*Now I have to live out a life for which you'll never care.*

Still here I wait and there's nothing I need
That I haven't needed from the beginning.
This October chill has replaced all the things

You could give me and the world will keep spinning.
My desire to know why they did what they did
Is fading with the green in the leaves;
The somethings I had hurt worse than the nothings
I always felt I should grieve.

The angels told me love was blind
But somehow I was left behind;
When the songs had run their course
Still I waited—now the source
Of all my troubles shows itself:
I had feared to know myself.
Why should I give them a dance
When they all chose to miss the chance?

*It's just another heart that I can't take for granted…*
*It's just another song that I'm not allowed to sing…*
*I'm just another dead corsage to you—you knew exactly what to do;*
*Now I have to try and ignore a piece of everything.*

There's snow out there on the year's horizon
Telling the world to turn.
There's snow in my head that's smothering desire
And telling the memories to burn.
Now they'll sit frozen on the very top shelf
While forgetfulness wears them away,
Blossoms of hope that are waiting to die
After somebody wore them a day.

Thoughts of them will come and go,
Thawing in summer and freezing in snow,
Slowly cycling out of existence,
Slowly abandoning all the persistence.

Autumn chimes will play the notes
And sing the lyrics conflict wrote.
Self pity keeps your mind in place
And lives to hide your life's disgrace.

*It's just another dance that I don't know the steps to...*
*It's just another tale that I'm not allowed to tell...*
*It's just another dead corsage to see among forgotten old debris;*
*Now you need to move on without me and know I wish you well.*

The volatile weather has worn me down,
Warm air turning to brisk.
More flowers are waiting to bloom underneath,
Unwilling to take the risk.
The echoing emptiness rests in my head
But the fire refuses to die.
Regret keeps trying to make an old case
But my eyes are refusing to cry.

I'm sure they never meant to teach me
What I learned—now they can't reach me.
Ease the mental fists of hate,
Embrace unwanted twists of fate;
Self pity earns us nothing more
Than torture at our sorrow's core.
Don't keep mementos from your past
Unless you want your future cast.

*It's just another day that I can't bring an End to...*
*It's just another light that I'm not allowed to find...*
*You're just another dead corsage to me, so turn around and let me*
*be*
*While I put the past in its grave and leave it all behind.*

# THE FUNERAL PROCESSION

Standing on the corner
In a busy part of town;
Wishing it was warmer
And staring at the ground.
Leaves just keep on falling;
It's their time of year.
Lovers keep on stalling
And wipe each other's tears.
Down the street it's coming,
Too slow for him to tell
Just if that solemn drumming
Is going to treat him well.
As the hearse draws closer
He sees who's inside
And that no one who knows her
Is paying any mind.
No one glances, no one cares,
No sign of any kind;
But then he sees they're unaware
Because it's in his mind.
He looks in through the window,
But only sees himself.
His thoughts can only swim, though,
In ways that he once felt...

*There goes the girl I thought you were,*
*There goes my wife.*
*My dignity, my sanity, my God,*
*There goes my life.*

Those leaves keep on falling;
It's their time of year.
Banshees keep on calling,
Reminders of his fear
That the only one who's dying
Is the one who sees the hearse,
Though death wins over crying
Through a lifetime of her curse.
She never meant to kill him,
But he's dying anyway.
Though yesterday she thrilled him,
He weeps today away.
He watches as it drives on
And knows now what's inside.
Nothing left to thrive on
But knowing he can't hide.
Down the street it's going,
And with it all his tears
For everything worth knowing
Of all those happy years.
When you can't go farther,
The sun can rise through pain.
While growing up gets harder,
It happens just the same…

*There goes my weakness down the road,*
*And with it all my fear.*
*Now to pay the debts I've owed*
*And start a brand new year.*

# THE WAY OF THE STAGE DIVE

There's an ominous glow at the front of our stages, put
there by people who want us in cages,
That gets reinforced when some cash changes hands
from the ones with the pull to the ones in the stands.
The paperwork says that it's for our security but all that
they've done is abolished the purity
Of anyone's thoughts who takes fire from the amps—
and stole the basic freedom from the minds in other
camps.
The primary source of our sad epidemic is that each
one of us has been willing to let it
Be taken for granted that we have our own lives and
have searched for acceptance everywhere but inside.
They say we need protection and race to assist us, ask
us for money and say evil missed us.
Our thoughts and our actions are all under scrutiny, so
now it's past time for an old-fashioned mutiny.

*Free will can still breathe if we're brave enough to leave*
*An example for those who most need the reprieve.*
*Situations require that we all return fire*
*At political rhetoric and big corporate liars.*

They'll steal your life savings if it means they can line
their own pockets with the money they get from the
fines

They impose on the people who work to get by while they win their elections with insults and lies.
They'll provide us with everything they say that we need—provided it lets them indulge in their greed
And they crank on the vise while they tell us they care and start figuring out how to tax us for air.
They boast about changes then hand us excuses we only accept 'cause we all feel the nooses
They tighten each time they approve a new law that says living should be more expensive for all.
They'll bury a knife in your back to the hilt and then twist 'till they see your stability wilt
And then they'll retract it, expecting applause, which you'll give them because you don't have any claws.

*There's no way around it—admit we've allowed it;*
*The solution is out there, we just haven't found it.*
*As long as we swallow incessantly hollow*
*Half truths then we'll never have our own paths to follow.*

Safety comes first at the shows that we see, but whatever happened to the way it used to be?
Lost in a tangle of law suits and blame, pushed to extinction by those who only came
To find out how we feel about good versus bad so they know what to tell the ones making the ads.
Bring back the recklessness, bring back the noise, bring back true rebellion, fill in the voids
They created somehow when they tore us apart— there's no better time than the present to start.
They can't see the chance if we rise and outshine them; they'll know we're still free if we join and remind them.
When you find yourself living outside of your means (not because of your choices, because of their schemes),

If you find yourself breaking your back to survive
despite your best efforts then take a stage dive.

*The rebels in the pit all know it; voices raised and clenched fists
show it—*
*Time has come to take a side and work to overthrow it.*
*The airwaves need to band and blare enough to make them stop
and stare—*
*While they think they're catching the collective unaware.*

It's about finding strength and a choice for the
choiceless, wages for the underpaid and voices for the
voiceless.
It's bending the rules to the point that they break and
embracing with pride the mistakes that we make
Under heat from the forces that raised us to think that
the only right way is to bow down and drink
Up the stories they tell about justice and salaries, cars
and celebrities, diamonds and calories,
How to get trim at an uncanny rate even though the
plans keep you in an inactive state.
It's about taking action and damning excuses and
planting the bombs because *they* lit the fuses.
To Hell with redemption and damn their salvation; your
Way shouldn't be someone else's creation.
The stage dive says what we feel without trying, but
thanks to complacency that art is dying.

*If there are any rebels left who'd see tomorrow turn the tide*
*Then make a fist today and tell them we don't want their
genocide.*
*All the things that made us strong are disappearing as I speak*
*And all the things that make them rich are gaining strength
because we're weak.*

*If we all want it better and brace for the weather then nothing they
do can ever weaken or sever the resolve of a million standing
together in the face of the tyrants for freedom forever.*

# RIVER GIRL

I had been around the world, maybe once, maybe twice,
I had seen hills of fire, I had seen caps of ice.
My lungs had had the pleasure of breathing clean air
And I had met a million people both dark skinned and
fair.
I had tried to climb Everest, I had walked the Great
Wall,
I had lived in the cities where the acid rain falls.
I had spent my life roaming the Earth, and unwisely
I thought that its people could no more surprise me
'Til on my way home, when I passed through a town
With a curious method to care for its grounds.
A welcoming sight, this quaint little 'ville,
It had put down its roots at the base of a hill.
And off near the outskirts where flowers were growing
A clear, gentle river was silently flowing.
The people were friendly, and as I passed through
I was asked if I'd stop for a minute or two.
Seeing no reason to rush out of town,
I decided it couldn't hurt to slow my pace down.
I was offered a meal just before I would leave
Of the finest ingredients your mouth would believe.
I thanked all my hosts for the food and well wishes
And asked them if I could help out with the dishes.
I needed to know to where I should deliver
The waste and they all pointed me toward the river.

"Just walk to the edge, just a quarter of a mile,"
I was told, "River Girl cleans it up with a smile."
"I'm sorry," I said, "I don't think that I follow;
Just who is this girl you claim likes to wallow
In trash left by others after every such meal?
Seems a little far fetched to be taken for real."
"You'll see," they all told me, "just go out and drop it;
The River Girl waits down the river and mops it."
"Does she live around here?" I asked of my hosts,
"Or are we talking about some unnatural ghost?"
"She's as real as the dinner you just got done eating,
But she's too busy cleaning to stop for a meeting."
"Has anyone seen her? Does she ever come through,
Or is this just a story your grandparents knew?"
One of the oldest then answered my questions
With a short but convincing local history lesson.
"My daddy told me, and his daddy told him,
That the River Girl lives in the river to swim.
If she sees something stray getting swept by the current
She cleans it right up like a good little servant."
"Good enough," I then told them, "I won't make a
fuss;
In your Tolkien-like legends and folklore I trust."
I carried the garbage straight down to the river,
But my eyes couldn't find their mysterious swimmer.
I looked down the bank and saw others from town,
Having finished their meals, each one throwing down
An armful of trash they had made at their feast,
But not one had a care or concern in the least.
With a sigh and a shrug I then followed my orders
And watched all my trash float down the town's border.
I couldn't quite make trash in the river belong,
So I spoke to myself about what might be wrong.
"The people who live here may simply not care,

But I wonder if there really is someone down there."
I walked for a day and a night and again,
'Til I finally stood at the long river's end.
And of all of the wonders I've seen in the world,
It's this that stays with me: there was no River Girl.
It emptied out into a large, vast expanse
And I watched more trash slowly make its advance
On the mouth of the river and then on forevermore
As it all found its way to some poor, foreign shore.
My suspicions confirmed, my hope torn asunder,
I stood by the river and stoically wondered
How many River Girls toil away
In the minds of her locals who think her a slave?
How many problems get dumped in a river
And forgotten thanks to a supernatural swimmer?
How many towns think this righteous and fair,
Not knowing there never was a River Girl there?
The River Girl is the most pleasant story around,
And we can keep looking, but she'll never be found.
When I made my way home by way of the sea,
The first thing I did was set my River Girl free.

## NEXT TO THE PIT

Nervous eyes in a pretty face—
They stand out for me as abruptly as silence in sound.
Nervous eyes have earned your space—
On an island surrounded by a sea made of long lost
crowds.

It truly is a grave injustice—
That those eyes can be wandering, still not having
found what they need.
You smiled but it barely missed—
It was brighter than the stage but too truthful for
anyone to see.

I want you to feel worthy and noticed—
I want you to know that the world can't tell you who
you are.
I want you to stay steady and focused—
I hope you do what you do and your dreams are all
aimed at the stars.

You guard your time extremely well—
And as honored as I am that you wanted to give it to
me,
Time itself in time will tell—
If our encounter was all that we both knew we wanted
it to be.

The timing of our gaze was wrong—
You offered a hand and I shook it but I couldn't hold
on.
So now we have to say so long—
We'll turn different ways and remember this as we go
on.

I'm sorry I can't know you better—
When the lights come on you'll be part of the past left
behind me.
So put what you felt in a letter—
And maybe some day when the fighting is done it'll find
me.

Someday when everything changes—
When our dreams are all shattered and reality has made
us both quit,
After all the bad thoughts and exchanges—
You can come back and find me; I'll always be next to
the pit.

# YOYU

I hope that the fog of the spiritual war will complicate
life to the point that I break.
With all my days numbered I count on impossible tasks
to impede every step that I take.
I hope that the day never comes when I find that it's
easy to steady my road-weary bones;
A failure indeed if I let myself think I deserve to be
anything past an unknown.
I hope that the struggle leaves no room for words and
my only clear choice is to live through my actions
And people will not understand what I am and I'll
always forgive their unwanted reactions.
The good in the best of us slowly will form as I force
myself past all my envious needs,
And my heart becomes tough as I work to accept the
disasters no matter how much it might bleed.
I'll aspire to live by a standard that others will scorn and
avoid every chance that they get;
I'll experience doubt many times but I won't ever waver
or slip once my mind has been set.
I won't fill my life with material things even though my
environment generates plenty;
I'll keep to the ground and remember to feel some
disgrace at my hunger when running on empty.
Always I'll rather lose fairly than win after cheating my
foe out of all of his strength,

So I never will fight any battles with salt even though it might lead to my failure at length.
I'll bear anything that I feel I should bear even though I can't bear anymore at the time;
Formless like water, I'll give it all up and no sign of my passing will be left behind.

*And as I near my End of days, I pray that I can fix my gaze*
*And that my beauty fades so I may better serve my cause.*
*And when the mirror shows my face, I pray that I have earned my place*
*And that my past disgrace will help me better see my flaws.*

May you find appreciation in unlikely places, where nothing is cherished and comfort is gone.
May you be a reminder to every lost cause that with every long night comes another still dawn.
I hope that the Fates find it fitting to give you the rest that you've earned and your story a sequel
And to look in the mirror is the only way left for one such as you to lock eyes with an equal.
Your integrity stands with a firmness of soul that the rest of the world has all but let die,
And your honesty lives like the breath in your lungs even though you've decided the world deserves lies.
May you never be compromised out of your faith in yourself by the ones still reluctant to see
That the very faith focused outside of themselves is exactly what keeps them from being set free.
May you strike when your reasons and feelings are strong and steady your hand when the time deems it right,
And remember to keep in perspective those feelings when voices inside say to run to the fight.

May all your decisions come quickly and keep to the
course that your spirit has found to be yours,
And hold to your courage in spite of the danger you
feel waiting for you behind the closed doors.
May the chords from the good in the best of our artistic
ventures preserve your ideal to The End,
And the changing winds never be stronger than your
resolution to always accept what life sends.
May you live in a Way that brings peace to the restless
and offer the falling a safe place to fall;
May you be the only one who rejoices at your End—
this is my most earnest wish for you all.

*And with our futures in our hands, I pray that we can take
command
And that we understand how much we still have left to lose.
And when the fear of loss is there I pray that we can be aware
For what we really care unless we want to die confused.*

# I AM THE PAIN

I look out the window at the pitch black of night
For the sounds that originate just out of sight.
A horror show slowly goes by, and I see
All the images shown are meant only for me.
Enough pain's in front to make a guy lose his mind;
God and The Revelation aren't far behind.
A girl named Lonely is bound up in chains
And marched by the Reaper; his hands on her reins.
Failure and consequence both rear their heads
As I hear the humiliating things that I've said.
A lifetime of lies is brought into view
And gets taken for granted by a world with no truth.
Out comes a man with an animal's stride,
Steering it all with a sadistic pride,
For it's all coming down and the only ones standing
Are those who I grew with, still reprimanding.

> *I am The Fear, and your tears are what give me my cheer;*
> *There's no way to race or outlive me.*
> *The time is so near when you'll face all the truth in your lies*
> *And beg for me to take out your eyes.*

These are the friends who stayed with me, and I,
In my moment of weakness, had failed to realize
That angels are not always sent down from God,

And demons do not always rise from the sod.
Funeral parties for loved ones are thrown
While soldiers of fortune write letters to home.
It's hard to hear voices that break due to violence,
But make no mistake—the dead are not silent.
The people I miss are engraving their names
On my door, leaving trails of hope, anger, and shame.
Traditions long gone and forgotten all pass
By the window, each stopping to stare through the
glass.
Out comes a man crying blood in the rain,
Summing up the long stories of anguish and pain
And it's all coming down one life at a time,
Leaving only my life for my friends to rewind.

> *I am The Sorrow; I'll borrow your taste*
> *For tomorrow and all the regrets you won't face.*
> *I love what you are, though—a boat caught in waves of*
> *the past*
> *And too scared to run a sail up the mast.*

On the night drags and I see, one by one,
All the tragic events that have left me undone.
Emotions run high, and the feverish sound
Of a temper lost makes my heart sink to the ground.
Loss of control and grudges against
What I love take meaning out of what was first meant.
Killers go by, chasing victims without
Any reason except their blind need to reach out.
There's fire that's burning injustice to Hell
And Heaven's ablaze with the rich clientele.
A scream at the truth of life's ways fills the sky
And collapsing are walls that kept mayhem inside.
Out comes a man with a bomb in his grip;
His words are suggesting that grip will soon slip

'Cause it's all coming down—but who's left to go?
Who's here to care about what they don't know?

> *I am The Fury, don't worry about plans, you just hurry*
> *And fly down the path you just ran.*
> *The truth is still blurry; I'm finished with figuring out*
> *How to handle a world with such doubt.*

The night is still young and a figure is falling
From space, all the way kicking, screaming, and calling
Out loud for the torment he feels to desist—
But there's no one to hear his shouts here in the mist.
Showers of bones that are broken are cast
Over kicks in the teeth, soaring back through the past.
The migraines they cause are only a blessing,
Hiding the years that are spent always guessing.
All over again my own thoughts are abusive,
My sanity threatened and my comfort elusive.
All over again I feel hours of pain,
Days of neglect, months and years of disdain.
Out comes a man missing half of his face
And half of his life he'll relentlessly chase,
While it's all coming down, his own peace of mind
And all the humanity he left behind.

> *I am The Pain, baby, rain in my head*
> *So insane that I won't believe all that's been said.*
> *I derailed the train that kept faith on its fake, charted*
> *course;*
> *All I want is a life of remorse.*

And into the future they all seem to go,
Just waiting for me to get up and let go
Of the fear and the pain and the sorrow I keep
With the fury I harbor each night as I sleep.
But only to give me some more do they wait,

Each knowing the course of my life and its fate.
Resigned to the things I should face past it all,
It's my choice to keep living and answer the call.
Alone with my instinct and life's resolution,
Preparing myself to serve all retribution,
I see definitions give way to the laws
Of what's real, always weakening the strength of their
claws.
Out comes a man who cannot be defined,
Defying the sense of what's real in my mind
When it's all coming down and I have to believe
In a reason for the life that I've chosen to lead.

> *I am The End; my friends are all gone*
> *And they send no regards as I face the next dawn.*
> *Alone here again, nothing new when I'm cold to the*
> *touch*
> *So it won't do to worry too much.*

These I was left with, so these are my friends:
The Sorrow, The Pain, Fear, Fury, The End.
Friends such as these can be hidden by blindness
Because it's so easy to not see their kindness
When it's all coming down, but it's still only right
That they'd be the emotions we take to the fight.
So I am The Pain, and I'm done feeling shame
At the thought of the world calling out my new name.

# HARLEQUINS AND MARIONETTES

The six rings of the circus have never failed to please;
It's easy to enjoy the show from outside looking in.
Performers smile at the crowd, all waving human hands;
Standing in the center of it all with evil grins.
Painted faces, strings attached, this isn't just a show,
Although the crowd is standing and applauding with respect.
A line is formed, and out come gymnasts, laughing at them all,
Involving all the people just to get the full effect.
Underneath the big top all the lights go out at once;
The grunts of shock and awe persist until the Master speaks.
"And now, the Harlequins of All Your Fears will entertain,
Refrain from screaming, and remember, never leave your seats."
The room stays dark until the center ring is lit up bright
In spite of all the people who are uttering remarks.
And as they're waiting for the show to start, the drum roll sounds,
Rebounding off the big tent walls in scattered, random arcs.

And out the first performer comes with animated strides,
Widely grinning as she surveys all the little girls.
Her mask is made of plastic and its face is frozen stiff;
She lifts a colored mirror to reflect her long, blonde curls.
Stage hands come out and pose her, twisting her in different ways;
The dazed look on her face suggests that this is all she knows.
They spread her legs and arch her back, but Plastic feels no pain;
Amazingly contorted limbs assure that anything goes.

> *Her glazing eyes seem crucified, nailed by lies they keep inside;*
> *Every motion of her hands demands that girls will do the same.*
> *Standing, dropping, kneeling, stopping just for playtime on the ride,*
> *Motions that the girls repeat are just rules of the game.*

The second Harlequin comes out running, waving both his hands,
Demanding the attention of the ones who won't behave;
Glaring through a mask of sorrow that he swears is joy,
The boys and girls, he says, will all fall to their unmarked graves.
His movements scare the children, but adults believe his words;
Encouraging them all to jump through narrow rings of fire,
He's balancing on stacks of books all sacred to the show;

And knowing how his speeches sound he knows what men desire.

> *Books are burning, fears are churning, mothers yearning for the stern*
> *Confirmation that their dreams and schemes will somehow raise the young.*
> *Everlasting life is just a knife that always keeps on turning,*
> *Making worse our mimics of the movements as we're stung.*

With somersaults and crouching dashes, out the third clown comes,
Among a ring of lions, roaring as he gets too close.
His clothes are drab, his face is painted black and green and brown,
Around his waist are hanging things that lions fear the most.
He puts his head into the mouth of one malignant beast,
A feast for any lion who decides that he should bite.
All the grown-ups follow suit as if they're tied to strings,
Which brings the lion's mouth down hard for nothing more than spite.

> *Please don't go, you have to know that it's all part of our great show,*
> *Every time he dies, we just replace the face on someone else.*
> *Do as he does, then you'll see that all your children need to grow*
> *And be the next to test the fates and wear that ammunition belt.*

Harlequin four is springing out, flashy as a Christmas morning,
Scorning all the others and their boring forms of entertainment.
Her brightly colored face and clothes can leave those watching wincing,
Convincing all those present that they never knew what sane meant.
Her flips are fun, she tumbles on the stage and hands out gold;
Untold mayhem comes alive, consuming all with lust.
The words she doesn't speak are all behind the mask she's wearing;
Glaring bright enough to keep from showing what's unjust.

> *It's alright for you to fight the splendid sights here every night,*
> *But when I pull your strings, young things, you all be sure to come.*
> *The world is big enough for everyone who still reserves the right*
> *To come out spending time and money just to see that they get some.*

The fans are all appalled at all these grotesque, twisted sights,
And rightly so demand to know who chartered the event.
But deep inside they all could tell that each one had a favorite,
And savored the performances they saw beneath the tent.
"Who would do this?" Someone asks, "Who would show this mess?

I demand my money back; my children got upset."
All the fans there nod together, feeling what he said;
Instead of cutting losses, they would rather build
regrets.
And up above the big top, floating high up in the sky,
The eyes of someone watching laugh at all the bright,
young things.
They all still have their demons, reasons just to make
some noise;
Still enjoyed by that same man, still pulling all their
strings.
Amidst the chaos, answers did find ways to those who
looked;
Who took the time to step back, placing greed up on
the shelves.
They found the strings that held them tight, yanked on
by the clowns;
They found the show's producers to be no one but
themselves.

## IN THE NAME OF THE FATHER

In a church not far from the towns you know,
A congregation listens as its faith starts to grow.
During the next hour, they're all born again
And determined to live by the words the preacher
sends.
But during the sermon, in the shadows of the mind
Are things that the people are unable to bind.
And in the back of the room, behind all the truths,
Demons get to their feet and start roaming the pews.

Dan sits to the left in his best Sunday suit
And while the sermon rolls on, is indefinitely mute.
He's thinking of the graves his new funding will dig,
A corporate American, a capitalist pig.
Mammon stops before him and looks through his eyes,
Flashes a grin, and Dan's faith quickly dies.
*"You know that the money you make hurts others,*
*But you keep making more at the cost of your brothers.*
*In the Name of the Father, you're here to confess,*
*But in the Name of the Father, your evil I bless.*
> *Neither Wisdom, nor Courage, nor Faith, nor Justice*
> *can keep you away from me.*
> *Neither Temperance, nor Hope, nor the status of your*
> *name can save your soul from me.*
> *My father Apolyon will indeed be most pleased."*

Chris sits on the left very near the back row
And the wits in his head have gone blunt long ago.
The id in his brain has freedom to creep
For while he's upright, he's also asleep.
Belphegor walks close, always dragging his heels,
And smiles when he's close enough to know what Chris feels.
*"You live your life slowly, without any care,*
*And you've come here thinking you'll be clean with one prayer.*
*In the Name of the Father, you want to be woken,*
*But in the Name of the Father, you're here to be broken.*

> *Neither Faith, nor Justice, nor Charity, nor Temperance*
> *can keep you away from me.*
> *Neither Wisdom, nor Hope, nor the dreams that you*
> *hide in can save your soul from me.*
> *My father Semihazah will indeed be most pleased."*

Peter is standing at the pulpit and speaking;
Looking out on the people his thoughts begin leaking.
He knows they're only reverent one hour in a week,
But still he keeps preaching, getting slapped on both cheeks.
Satan stands behind him and feels what's inside,
And Peter feels frustration and anger start to rise.
*"In the black of your heart you wish them ill will,*
*And all their hypocrisy makes you want to kill.*
*In the Name of the Father, you're here to spread word,*
*But in the Name of the Father, the truth becomes blurred.*

> *Neither Hope, nor Justice, nor Courage, nor Wisdom*
> *can keep you away from me.*
> *Neither Charity, nor Faith, nor the Second Coming*
> *Kingdom can save your soul from me.*
> *My father The Devil will indeed be most pleased."*

Amy sits on the right near the front of the mass,
Admiring herself in her small, reflective glass.
Adjusting her hair, making sure that her face
Is gorgeous enough to make men want a taste.
Lucifer sits next to her on her pew
And finds Amy's beauty doesn't reach all the way through.
*"You see yourself a bright star among women*
*Whose hearts are clean, while your thoughts are forbidden.*
*In the Name of the Father, you want to be pure,*
*But in the Name of the Father, you've come here to lure.*
> *Neither Courage, nor Charity, nor Temperance, nor*
> *Hope can keep you away from me.*
> *Neither Faith, nor Justice, nor the beauty of your face*
> *can save your soul from me.*
> *My father Belial will indeed be most pleased."*

Nichole likes to sit on the right side mainly,
But she can't seem to take her green eyes off of Amy.
She wants her white smile and her long, perfect legs,
But knows she can't have them despite how she begs.
Leviathan sees Nichole's eyes while he walks,
And knows in one instant that it's Amy they stalk.
*"You're blessed with a life most people would grab,*
*And all you can think of is what you don't have.*
*In the Name of the father, you want to be ready,*
*But in the Name of the Father, your green eyes burn steady.*
> *Neither Temperance, nor Courage, nor Wisdom, nor*
> *Charity can keep you away from me.*
> *Neither Justice, nor Faith, nor your near-perfect life can*
> *save your soul from me.*
> *My father Sammael will indeed be most pleased."*

Mike always sits at the back of the room,
Ashamed that his weight won't fit into the pews.
He tries to let Peter fill him up with good news,
Just the same, later on, he gets filled with good food.
Beelzebub hovers over him like a mischievous wight
And gives him more hunger to further his plight.
*"You're so thick even I can't reach your soul.*
*Your body is a temple, but you can't take control.*
*In the Name of the Father, you come here to wane,*
*But in the Name of the Father, all you do is gain.*

> *Neither Charity, nor Courage, nor Hope, nor Wisdom*
> *can keep you away from me.*
> *Neither Faith, nor Temperance, nor your good intentions*
> *can save your soul from me.*
> *My father The Dragon will indeed be most pleased."*

Sam sits on the left with his wife and his daughter,
But not glancing right gets harder and harder.
It's Amy, sitting pretty, who his eyes want to see.
It's Amy, wearing red, who he wants his wife to be.
Asmodeus feels heat and tracks it to its source,
Finds herself in front of Sam and gets down on all
fours.
*"You already love, but you can't help your feelings.*
*If you weren't in church you'd go over to her kneeling.*
*In the Name of the Father, you want to refuse her,*
*But in the Name of the Father, you're going to use her.*

> *Neither Wisdom, nor Temperance, nor Justice, nor*
> *Charity can keep you away from me.*
> *Neither Courage, nor Hope, nor your pure-hearted wife*
> *can save your soul from me.*
> *My father Azazel will indeed be most pleased."*

The demons return to the rear of the church,
All having completed their unholy search.
And looking out over the worshipping crowd
All seven demons in unison say aloud:
*"In the Name of the Father they misunderstand,*
*They're afraid to take command, won't follow His plan.*
*In the Name of the Father they all go to war,*
*They fight with each other, they close all their doors.*
*In the Name of the Father they look down and condemn,*
*They all think they're true, that Heaven only loves them.*
*In the Name of the Father they come here to cry,*
*And in the Name of the Father they live in their lies."*

Six turn to leave, but Lucifer stays behind;
There's one final thought that still troubles his mind.
*"They all want to be at the next kingdom's dawn,*
*But in the Name of the Father, the Message is gone."*

## (Social Anorexia)

Our values stripped her of her clothes, but it's all right,
for we all know
That as a girl you just can't make it without displaying
yourself naked.
We make her bad and act obscene while we look
through magazines
And stare into those big, brown eyes while telling all
our filthy lies.

When did she ever have a chance?  Her life has been a
fake romance.
When did she give up on love?  If shallow fits, then
wear the glove.
What else is there to expect when the world breathes
down your neck
And makes you think you won't go far unless you meet
that social par?

Look this way, laugh this way, walk, talk, and act this
way,
Bend this way and pose this way and we'll make you a
star someday.
And how effective are they all at getting her to heed
that call?
"Tell me please," she turns to say, "How cheap should
my love be today?"

So dance this way and play this way, get drunk, get high, you're cool that way,
Feel this way and think this way, do your hair and nails this way,
Read a lot on how to be hot and we won't care if you are or not
'Cause if you're willing to do what we say, then sexy, you'll be big someday.

Love what you have and want what you don't, take yourself shopping each week so you won't
Start to think that you're all by yourself in this life; as long as you're rich, my dear, you're all right.
Take these pills so you won't get fat; six easy steps and you'll never go back.
Take extra care that you wear the right clothes and learn how to striptease from someone who knows.

And strip this way and spread this way, do whatever but do it our way.
If you don't want to do it, do it anyway and baby, you'll be a star someday.
We don't care what you think you should see or what kind of person you think you should be,
And it's all right that you lost all your dreams 'cause this life raises your self esteem.

Up in the penthouse, above all the noise, a team of six people just watch and enjoy.
There in the room, untouched by fear, they don't feel pain and they can't see the tears.
Bulbs keep flashing, the ink is still wet and every day more are caught in the net.

As the countdown begins they all pause to say, *"How can we market their lives today?"*

Eight by eight they won't say no since seven at a time makes such a great show.
Six by six they're all made to give as five by five they die as they live.
Four at once make love through war while three by three their egos soar.
Two by two their smiles shine… but one by one they'll fall in line.

*"We always know what they love best because we say to ignore the rest,*
*But now our intake starts to climb because our 'product' is firmly in mind.*
*They'll love our way and date our way, look toward us to know the right way.*
*The target age group just might fall, but they'll still want to heed our call.*

*This one here could be a star, provided she lets us go too far.*
*Let her hair down and trim up her waist and find out how she performs in bad taste.*
*We can excuse that uneven tan as long as she spreads just as wide as she can.*
*Make all her wishes come true in one day and in no time at all she'll forget yesterday."*

In a room in a house in a town they don't know, a young man sits as his tears start to flow.
He's staring at a picture of a girl overhead, recalling how once they had planned to be wed.

Alone in the corner except for her stare, he's haunted by visions of men who don't care.

He's holding the picture he carried everywhere and clenching his teeth since life won't be fair.

Despite all his pain he swears he'll be strong as he's blaming himself for all that went wrong.

He's staring at a picture of a girl fully clothed and thinking of all that he's now come to loathe.

Alone in the corner he wishes her well, not ready to admit that his love prefers Hell.

He knows that she's gone, even though he still cares— hey, nobody told him that life would be fair.

## DEAR JESUS
(A Life in the Day of a Deity)

Now I lay me down to sleep,
I pray the Lord can't see me weep.
When Satan comes upstairs to find me,
Please, dear Jesus, come and hide me.
Help me sleep without a sound
So through the night I won't be found.
In the darkness he'll come creeping,
Reaching for me while I'm sleeping.
From the closet he can hear me—
Please, God, please don't let him near me.
Help me conquer all my fright
As I kneel and pray tonight.
When mommy reads to me I'm wary
Since her stories always scare me.
I try hard to be so good
And do what Jesus says I should.
*Fear and fire crowd my dreams but mommy makes me hush my
screams.*
*Time goes by and I will grow and be a man who sin won't know.*

I'm praying to the Father and His Son and Holy Ghost.
Many come to church to pray but I come here the
most.
There are many things I need from You if You're still
with me—

So many wishes that I hope that You'll see fit to give me.
I feel I've earned attention since I'm praying all the time,
And ask the church—I've been the best as far as giving tithe.
I really need that law to pass so I can keep my land;
I'd like to keep my boat on that half acre as I planned.
I think my daughter's been up late and sneaking out at night—
Please guide her to the truth, my Lord, and make her see the light.
She's found herself a troubled friend who doesn't praise Your Name,
And while he does seem nice enough I hate him just the same.
My wife could use another room for all her odds and ends
And so I need some extra cash—whatever You can send.
And please don't ever let her know my whereabouts at night;
My mistress needs my help, O Lord, she needs You in her life.
*Thank You Jesus, thank You God, for giving me Your blessed nod,*
*I'll never let you down, my King, as long as I can have these things.*

I get so tired of looking back and knowing my missteps never ceased,
But through it all I could have sworn that all I felt was inner peace.

I don't know what to think about these dreams that
haunt me every night
In which there's someone telling me that I have yet to
find my sight.
It all went wrong at every turn that ever mattered—
now I need
To know exactly what You planned and how You saw
it helping me.
When I go out in public now I always have to hide my
face;
My daughter openly defied my wish and married out of
race.
My wife found out about my fling and never let me live
it down
And now I have to check and see when I go out if she's
around.
I thought last year I heard You say to put my savings all
on Red.
You told me that You'd make me rich no matter what
my spouse had said.
But that fell through, and then the only choice I had
was very clear—
I took the sign You gave me, God, and hit the streets
for one full year.
I spread Your Word throughout the city, living off of
what I found,
But people simply passed me by as though I never
made a sound.
*Lord, I don't know what to say to sinners when they turn away.*
*Jesus, by Your holy light, I beg, make everything all right.*


I made my way back home in time but now I can't see
any colors;

All my world is black and white and everything around
me shudders.
Both the children I have left have grown to hate my
very name
In just as many ways as I found all through life to shift
their blame.
Dear Jesus, can't You hear me? Aren't You with me?
Won't You make it stop?
I think that I've lost touch with who I am and I just
want to drop
These last few years down through a void and not
believe they ever were;
The things I've done to please You, Lord, I can't
confess they're so absurd.
All Your symbols and Your maybes made my daughter
kill her babies—
Now she swears while she's in prison thanks to her
You'll soon be risen.
All those voices that she heard are now repeating every
word
That over these last years they've said, but now they're
all inside *my* head.
Long ago my life was wrecked and now all sinners go
unchecked;
I know I'll never get Your reasons—still I'll praise You
all four seasons.
After all, I've done what's right—I know I've earned
eternal life,
And when the Father's Voice commands You'll raise
me up and wash my hands.
*Now I lay me down to sleep, I pray the Lord can't see me weep.*
*Who in all their time would say a righteous life could be this way?*

# I CAN SEE YOU

There's a little girl crying by herself in the corner;
The little girl's crying 'cause she lives in disorder.
Her life has been rough and she feels overlooked,
And she misses the things that the other kids took.
She waits for the favor she swears that she's owed
And she waxes romantic about the betrothed
Who she thinks is still out there just dying to see
If their love can be all that she wants it to be.
But her love only comes through drama and fights
And her confidence shakes when you turn on the lights,
And she talks about honor and everything right
As she borrows your money and bids you goodnight.

*Little girl fantasies with little girl names,*
*Playing with her baby dolls little girl games,*
*Keeping all the memories in little girl frames,*
*I can see you, Little Girl, there's no one else to blame.*

Her memory long ago blocked her abuses;
Her throat has gone dry thanks to all those excuses.
Her mind lost an edge that it never really had;
Her eyes stay wet because she's always really sad.
It's a shame the world thinks that her fix is her fault,
It's a shame the world turned all her sugar to salt.
She shouldn't have to deal with the things that we do;

Had the world helped her she might have seen it
through.
It's a race to the finish and we all slowed her down;
When she needed some luck it was nowhere around.
The good hand she was dealt just didn't pan out;
The fortune she was granted either left or ran out.

*Alone in the corner throwing little girl tantrums,*
*Defending herself with her little girl phantoms,*
*Little girl words used just to enchant them,*
*But I can see you, Little Girl, and I won't sing your anthems.*

She's everything everyone wants and will look
Like a damsel straight out of a fairytale book
If that's what she thinks the crowd wants her to be;
She'll show you whatever you might want to see.
She gets what she wants from the wandering eyes
Of the men who are spoken for—men who have wives,
And her only concern is herself when she tries
To engage them in acts that would bring their demise.
She thinks she's a rarity—she's earned a better place;
Her sorrow for herself is written all across her face.
But I can see the mayhem she's been leaving in her
wake;
I can see you, Little Girl, and I can see you're fake.

*Little girls love to latch on to what's new,*
*Little girl reasons leave truth black and blue,*
*Little girls never want the truth to be true,*
*Which little girl is familiar to you?*

# TRYING AND FAILING

A decade of trying and failing
To cure all the things which are ailing
Our otherwise harmless intentions
Puts body and mind in dissention.
After we got what we wanted,
Duty stopped being confronted;
It's easy to slip when we're offered
A break from the problems we've authored.

*Failure has made me so tainted,*
*Yet the evil in me goes unstated—*
*My worthiness left with my freedom of will and my strength and I*
*find myself hated.*

Our thoughts of changing the world
As we grow become jaded and swirled
As others begin to show us
That they don't even care to know us.
We can't help but see our time wasted
When we finally see that we chased it—
A dream that was worthy of taking
From the demons we spent our time making.

*Failure has opened my eyes*
*To the evil in me that I hide—*

*All that I reached for was truth and a right without wrong but I only found lies.*

We all have the same choice to make,
We all have the same risk to take
On this road to The End we're all walking;
The trek never starts with our talking.
There never is shame in our trying;
The shame lies only in lying
To ourselves about what we deserve
And the effort we held in reserve.

*Failure has given me drive,*
*Still the evil in me will survive—*
*The mission to fight its intent will continue until I'm no longer alive.*

Step out and see what you're missing,
Roll the bone dice and stop wishing
For destiny to turn up and find you,
For the world to start getting behind you.
And keep yourself out of your way,
For your evil will come out to play,
And don't shy away from perfection;
Stare down the accusing reflection.

*Failure has made me a man,*
*Now the evil in me understands—*
*That it won't have to die though the standards are high and I won't entertain its demands.*

# SILVERDANCE

I'm dancing with No One, but I ask just the same
If my partner will ever remember my name.
I'm dancing with No One, as I have all this time,
Even though my denial was my only crime.
My blood moves faster in and out of my heart,
My sneaking suspicion is our signal to start.
Our temperatures rise and we enter a trance
As myself and No One begin our love dance.
*Don't try to save me 'cause I asked for this dance—I asked to see*
*this side of what the hopeful call romance.*
*Don't try to help me 'cause you don't know the steps—you don't*
*know the remedy or secrets I've kept.*

It tends to look different each time it's performed;
It depends on your limberness and how long the storm
Has to creep on the skyline before moving in.
So many dancers out there never win
Though the steps are so basic and easy to learn
'Cause sometimes the dance floor can numb you or
burn.
The best way to practice the sinister art
Is to make yourself scarce when you see the dance start.
*If you try to cut in you'll get caught in a sin that isn't your fault*
*and they'll leave with the win.*
*Just let dance play and let come what may and I hope that you all*
*emerge winners someday.*

73

Step 1—give yourself over to love;
Step in very close so your partner can shove
You away for step 2, where you both exchange blows
In whatever manner you decide you both know.
For steps 3 and 4 you both need to bleed
Then fall to the ground, too proud to concede.
Step 5 stands you up, but it's pointless to do
Because No One is a better dancer than you.
*And somewhere beyond your threshold of pain, beyond all the
laws that have kept your mind sane,
Something behind your eyes will let go as those thin scarlet streams
become a silver flow.*

Step 6 is the worst—your feet lose the rhythm
As you try at all costs to sew up the schism
The dance has created but it just can't be done,
And with a violent twist you start back at step 1.
You'll be twisting joints and you'll hate all the screams,
But you'll love all the heat brought on by the steam.
You'll finish it off and you'll savor the pain
As the blood starts to mix with the silver in your veins.
*They'll try to understand, but they'll never relate to the feelings
that have put you in your masochistic state.
They'll try to come near you, but don't take their love—don't
take their sympathy or help from above.*

After years of denial, I'm now very sure
That we are what we are, none sinners, none pure.
To hide who we are from the world is a crime;
Our nature will always come out in due time.
So be careful when we dance; I'll be quick to attack,
But only if you promise to hurt me right back.
We keep asking partners and answering calls
Because No One is the most brutal dancer of all.

74

*Whichever position you decide that you'll take will never really justify all 6 mistakes.*
*The guilt that will fall finds neither one more; we all leave the same silver tracks on the floor.*

Love can hit like a fist and it dances with blades
'Till the steel in your thoughts flashes all different shades.
It's a magnet for pain and the violence complex
Is as close to your mind as your body is to sex.
We don't understand why we feel like we do,
And we don't really know how to explain it in truth.
But for many long years the disease won't leave,
And we won't know which side to believe.
*And I'll just keep on dancing, seeing through my silver eyes and hoping deep inside that someday all my silver dies,*
*And when it does someone is there to catch me when I fall, and the silver truth is clear... I never won after all.*

# THE AFFLICTION

At last by yourself, you can turn off the phone;
The truest of friends never leave you alone.
The truest illusions are those you employ,
And the truest afflictions are those you enjoy.
It comes seeping in through the chinks in your armor
And raises some questions while starting to garner
Resolve you've established to turn it around;
With a whimpering sound you fall back, you give
ground.
And look, here she comes, your princess in white,
Your prize at The End of a long, moral fight.
It seems only right that she'd go to the loser;
The strength of a winner can always refuse her.
But what's to refuse when there's no one to see you?
Why be responsible when nobody needs you?
Close the door and take a look at what the master
brought;
Take one more and self control is just an afterthought.

*But what if the dead can see you?*
*What if your secrets get laid bare?*
*What if all the friends you had were never really there?*

*What if the door was open?*
*What if they saw you every time?*

It's a long, long night on a cold, cold floor
And the evil within you has settled the score.
Your weakness has once again made enough room;
The self was the bride and impulse the groom.
Too many occurrences now to excuse,
Control an illusion you never could use.
A measure of pride might be found where you lie
But the shame in your heart is too great to deny.
Forever you've fought it; forever you've failed—
The rest of life's struggles have long since paled
When compared to the master who now makes you
kneel
And the mistress who tells your insides what to feel.
It's hard to recover but your head knows you should—
Defeat has just never felt so damn good.
Again ripped apart but can't manage to weep;
The false angels are coming to put you to sleep.

*Is this what you've been working for?*
*Are you sure no one's around?*
*What if you went too far tonight and this is how you're found?*

*What if you die while sleeping?*
*What are they going to see?*
*Will the legend you made get buried with the person you tried to*
*be?*

The sunrise has found you again without pride,
For the sweet rush had ended along with the ride.
And now that it's over a part of you stays
On the floor while the rest of you searches for ways

To hide from the light coming in through the window;
There's no way to truly hide all the night's sins, though.
The rug feels like shackles, the blankets like pain,
The lamentations in your head are driving you insane.
You don't need to open your eyes to confirm
That your angel has once again left you to squirm
On the hook that she baited with promises broken
And pleasing thoughts now and forever unspoken.
She's left you again as she does every time;
Your time has been wasted again on the crime.
You indulge in the freedom to let yourself play;
Ironically, you're here because your freedom flew away.

*Do you remember the beginning?*
*Are you dying in between?*
*What will you have to say when this affliction is clearly seen?*

*Can you see The End from here?*
*Are you really trying to change?*
*Is there nothing left for you to try? No chance to rearrange?*

*Will you ever win the battle?*
*Can you find your lost free will?*
*Or is the affliction now too strong, a small price to pay for the thrill?*

# WHEN DIAMONDS MAKE YOU CRY

Life is shining, living's fun, you're loved by all your
friends;
Discomfort seems like just a dream, your smile never
ends.
Your problems drift so far away, storm clouds won't fill
the sky;
The ins and outs of daily life can never run you dry.
People want to be you, want to know you, and you'll
find
There's nothing hard that you can't take head on or
from behind.
Air fare takes you far away to where bad times won't
follow;
Pills and plastic make you numb when love's too hard
to swallow.
*Life will never cause you pain, your passion never dies;*
*Bows and boxes fill your dreams when diamonds make you cry.*

You'll be there as your children grow and give them all
the best
While all they know is how to take, ignoring all the rest.
It's hard to face the man outside your car while at the
light;
But oh, it's so damn easy to believe that he's alright.
Life drags on, and still you laugh, forever in denial;

The price of your love far outweighs the value of your smile.
Life gets dull, but all your wealth won't build you any bridges;
Nor will that ring that's on your hand be granting any wishes.
*Lust is never lost on you, your lover won't deny*
*That you're the best he's ever had when diamonds make you cry.*

What you want is out of reach, now shopping's just a chore;
You'll never find just what you want when all you want is more.
Your life is now an ice storm and you'd kill to find some gloves;
You sold your warmth for diamonds to a man who dealt false love.
And now you just keep grinning, hoping everything will change;
But never once admitting that your peace is out of range.
All your glitter shines so bright you'll never get to see;
The things that matter most in life come to us all for free.
*The mirror never makes you face the lies inside your eyes;*
*And there's no truth you can't escape when diamonds make you cry.*

# A BLISSFUL NAPALM DEATH

Let me fantasize about the lies you've put before my
eyes
And tell me how unwise I'd be to shake off what the
ruse implies.
Emphasize to me how much the lives of others need
that prize.
Improvise a way into my house and show me lines of
data
All designed to make me blind and hate the side across
the line.
Make me realize how much fun it is to camp out under
hostile skies
And show me nothing of the rise that comes with
pushing foreign lives
Into the vines of lies we make so we can try to
capitalize;
I want to be one of the guys with weekends off and
seven wives
In seven places, all with knives of hope stuck in their
sides and faces.
I'll go flying anywhere you like as long as I'm not dying;
Crying for the campus life I thought I'd be applying.
*Having fun and fitting in are worth more than my breath;*
*So let me be the first to march to a blissful napalm death.*

I was told I'm on vacation; now all of my mind's elation

Shatters all my concentration while I show up at the station.
Feeling like an imitation man and knowing my creation
Came from computation experts doesn't help my aggravation.
Someone stop this contemplation, please, show me my dedication
Matters more than realizations of our capitalization.
Show me that this confrontation's what I want; these implications
Of my own wrong confirmations make it hard in this vocation;
Giving all my dedication as per someone's calculations.
And through it all, I don't know why I can't find my salvation.
Provocation seemed to be the way to go, but exclamations
Of resistance and damnation fill the skies above these nations.
*Fighting for the right ideals is worth more than my breath;*
*So let me be the next to march to a blissful napalm death.*


I gave my life up for my leader, praying for him so he'd stay
And find a way to bring us to our victory one day.
What can I say?  I gave away my life so we could end this play
Of sand of clay with no delay but still we're out here every day.
I don't have to be afraid, for God is with me, I've been saved,
But why will He not save me now from this disgusting fray?

No vacation here… just pain while we're marching through the rain
That they wished on us; dying screams are driving me insane.
Soldiers all get rearranged and told that if they ever change
That stranger things have happened to important men who lost their way.
But still I'll leap without a light; I don't care if I was right.
The sight of blood is all I know and napalm burning bright.
*My life meant more the moment I gave this country my last breath;*
*So let me always march on toward that blissful napalm death.*

# THE MOTIVATION OF ALL EVIL

What can you find in a nice, hot bath on a grey
afternoon in storm's aftermath?
What can you find in holiday cheer and in special
events that bring family near?
It's what children get from a good bedtime story, and
what gardeners find in a fresh morning glory.
It's what couples find in their first slow dance and
intimate moments in their first romance.
It's the very same thing we can get from vacations and
what children get from their harmless creations.
It can also be found in erotic sensations, and even in
triumph and a good day's elation.
It's what parents get from a baby's conception and
what a bride finds at her wedding reception.
Walks in the park make it come back around, along
with delight seeing Easter eggs found.
Its symptoms are laughter, charity, and joy—its signs
are success, marriage, and toys.
It makes itself known in compliments given and all the
nice cars that are purchased and driven.

It's also what dictators get from the world, and what
rapists take from the sounds of young girls.
It's what drives a sadist to make himself bleed; it's what
makes us all live with more than we need,

The reason a murderer wants to kill more and the reason a man spends his nights with a whore.
It's why loving husbands will cheat on their wives and why they insist on persisting with lies.
It's what makes an addict crave all of those hits, and what drives lovers to sensual fits.
It's why we go out and get six figure jobs and why our opinions can quickly form mobs.
It's why we don't have the same passion for thinking that we have for our clubs, cars, parties, and drinking.
Everyone wants it, and everyone stares in the eyes of who gives it, all hoping they'll share
The portion they've found in their gifts and careers, in the jewelry they wear as they cry happy tears.
Always they chase, but never to find it, always they find themselves falling behind it.

The truth is that those who don't have it can give it, those who don't want it can't help but to live it,
Those who reach for it will never forgive it the Pain it will cause them—so tell me, what is it?

# JUSTICE IN WINTER
## (The Goddess of Wind and Rain)


Deep in the woods off a long, winding road, and
finding no reasons for where she now lay
Was a broken young woman half buried in snow, just
married, half clothed in torn rags and the gray
Of the season that later would prey on her heart and
remain there until she had seen her last day.
Dismayed eyes spoke of betrayal and hurt and had
frozen, uncertain of why she was slain
In a portrait of ice and without any warning, but
morning would yield all the answers she'd need.
If only she'd known of the meeting of late she might
not have died there under the tree.
But as is often the case, we see everything clearer in the
mirror when everything's done and behind us.
When life gets too warm and cozy it goes without
notice until something tragic reminds us.


*All the world around her now had bound her down to watch her
shake,*
*Dying with the light of day but trying hard to stay awake.*
*Silent stillness made her numb and deaf and dumb to everything*
*Except the burn of frost on skin and Lady Winter's icy sting.*
*No one there to even care or listen to her awful story,*
*Winter claimed her rigid frame and stole her breath in all its
glory.*

*On the floor of nature's house, a mouse without a chance in Hell,*
*Our heroine's dying wish was for the world to know her story*
*well.*

And her story begins, as these stories often do, with a
blue pair of eyes that weren't hers and a kiss
From a beauty queen aimed at her husband one night
when the sight of her made him feel physical bliss.
Standing in the corner with long, blonde hair, who
would dare turn her down if she shot him a glance?
Rare is the man who throws water on the fire within
when the liar within wants to dance.
So there in a smoky bar were all the seeds planted, and
frantic had been the ensuing night's crime.
His spouse was forgotten as soon as he entered her
bedroom to take his life off of his mind.
Now, what does a beauty queen get from this game?
It's the same sad story since love was invented.
Was it maybe the ring that he wore on his hand that
demanded her envy and what she intended?

*Our heroine was cast away if ever there was less a reason;*
*If only for a little while she lost her love in that cold season.*
*While she waited patiently at home he had to do his thing;*
*One night out without his bride had made him curse his wedding*
*ring.*
*He had to have that beauty queen who screamed with pleasure at*
*the touch*
*Of vows misplaced and love disgraced—hidden faces carry such.*
*No sincere apology can keep the deed from being done.*
*No amount of second chances justifies the late night fun.*

The beauty queen showed up in town after others had
found out about what she did and had chased

Her off to another small part of the world where all of
her pearls still seemed in good taste.
She never much cared for the ones on the prowl; those
settled down were the ones she preferred.
It was they who would give the most sport but resort to
submitting in the end with the rest of the herd.
Her eyes were the color of sexy except when she
needed to hide them to cover her shame.
With hair and a body to match, she could latch on to
any excuse that would help deflect blame.
At every chance given she turned up the heat with the
sun soured sweetness of one who can't wait
For all of the foreplay to pay for itself in any way likely
to keep them out late.

*Such a one had landed, reprimanded by the fates that followed*
*Town to town to hold her down and fill the voids in hearts she'd*
*hollowed.*
*Still she carried on with theft and left the loveless by the way,*
*But no one let her know she had to go before she got away.*
*Least of all the men befriended after dark in late night hours;*
*Such a one had landed, stalking neighborhoods like one who*
*scours*
*Like a fox in search of hens, bending wills with all her charms*
*And killing fills the empty space behind her face and in her arms.*

Eric and Donna were still getting used to sharing a
roost and preparing to live
Out the rest of their lives with each other and love one
another with all that they knew how to give.
They'd only been married a couple of weeks; neither
had reason to seek something else.
Their story was classic—one morning they met at their
college of choice and both of them felt

From the start it was destined, a love preordained;
nothing remained of the void that had captured
Their lives until then—much more than just friends and
the journey since then had been nothing but rapture.
Ideas for the wedding had already formed by the time
they had graduated; plans had been drawn
For the house they would share, the colors it would
wear and the land they would buy and the size of the
lawn.

*When school was done, they moved up north into a decent, mid-
sized town
Near a mountainous region of the country; there they settled down
And found a piece of ground that they could build on somewhat
near the city
So that Eric wouldn't have to drive too far to make his hard-
earned living.
Thoughts of children came soon after; Donna factored in the cost
And what it meant to be a parent, and apparently she thought
That it was something they could do and viewed the future being
bright.
So without tarry they got married; ever since she held him tight.*

The first few weeks were the dream they had seen in
their minds when they thought about how it would be;
Eric made a living and Donna kept giving her love to
the man who had set her heart free.
His job was in the city—an easy eight to four and he
swore that it couldn't get better than this.
Once he was settled he thought it would do them some
good to get out of the house for a bit.
Upon getting home he told Donna his thoughts, but
she fought the idea, saying, "Some other time.

My mother's expecting a call and the walls in the
kitchen need painting, but I wouldn't mind
If you took yourself out and got used to the town—
drive around for awhile then tell what you see.
Come back with some sights and then maybe the next
night I'll go; you need a break much more than me."

*Eric waved goodbye and told his wife that he might be out late;*
*Without a destination he could easily drive across the state.*
*In his car he climbed and down the driveway he had started off*
*To see the city, leaving pretty Donna back to mind the loft.*
*Eric drove for hours, combing streets and hoping he could find*
*A place where he and Donna could relax and spend their idle*
*time.*
*Soon a bar appeared, not far from all the busy city lights;*
*He'd step inside and then collide with fate that frozen Winter*
*night.*

When he got inside, the room looked too dim and he
almost turned on a whim and went out.
But after a second of taking it in, the place sort of
beckoned him in and his doubt
Was erased when he noticed how cozy the space was—
nothing too loud and nothing too bright.
He climbed up the stairs to the story above and he
thought of his love, for the place was just right.
In the corner he saw a girl drumming her fingers and
lingering on with her head on her fist.
She seemed to be waiting for someone; she kept
breathing deeply and checking the watch on her wrist.
Eric just watched as she stood up and slithered away
from the table to sit at the bar.
She looked over at him and instantly lust overtook him
and she said, "I know what you are.

*I know what you desire; you're a liar if you say you don't.*
*You're thinking I'm a stranger and a danger but I swear I won't*
*Do something you don't want me to; up front with you is all I'll be.*
*I'll save you from that prison you've created with that wedding ring."*
*Eric saw her eyes were blue and of his head no trace remained.*
*His wife forgotten, Eric shockingly proclaimed, "I need your name."*
*"Ashley," said the stranger, "and if you don't mind me saying so,*
*One who married young as you is sure to not have much control.*

"You rushed into marriage and thought you were set,
but I'll bet you don't realize just what you've been missing.
A girl such as yours is still only a whore whose
delusional mind won't reveal what she's wishing.
The girl must be done with experiencing life; she wants
to be somebody's wife so she never
Again has to fail at our glamorous game—command
her to wait and stay with me forever.
I know of a cabin up north we could have in an instant,
and there we could spend a few weeks.
We'd hide from the cold and the truth would be told
about what kind of woman you really do need."
Something hypnotic had made him psychotic and Eric
decided he wanted this girl.
The blue in her eyes was so mesmerizing; it promised
desire and asked for the world.

*Just before he spoke agreement, Ashley seemed to think again.*
*Knowing that she had him trapped, the beauty saw the chance to bend*

*Another will to grant her wish so she could do what she did best—*
*Take some loving, cause some losing, leave abusing to the rest.*
*"There's one thing you have to do if you want me to take you home.*
*If you want me and all my love you have to help me kill your own."*
*Eric thought it over with a mind he lost and couldn't claim,*
*Thinking on her words and how they sounded so completely sane.*

Eric and Ashley checked into a room where she filled his light head with advice about love
And why he rushed into marriage while Donna was carrying on back at home with her dishwashing gloves.
Morning came quickly and Donna woke early, certain her husband came home overnight.
But searching the house for a sign of him wasted her time, for Eric was nowhere in sight.
She got in her car and drove into the city, concerned about something she couldn't divine
And at last found his car outside of the bar but no others were with it at such an odd time.
The parking lot empty, she practically ran to the door and began to fear something had come
That would tear her away from her husband; she prayed that the culprit would never destroy love so young.

*At first relieved she found him there upstairs and that he'd been unharmed,*
*She looked again and saw his friend and felt there might be cause for alarm.*
*Walking to the table she was barely able to hide her fears;*
*When at last she spoke she had to blink away the welling tears.*
*She tapped her husband on the shoulder, trying to ignore the stare*

*That Ashley shot her way and told herself she shouldn't even care*
*About what someone else would think; she wanted Eric back at*
*home.*
*She told him nervously how hard it was to spend the night alone.*

The light in his eyes was strange when he introduced
Ashley, infused with a hypnotized glaze
And Donna was cordial enough, but repeated that
morning had come and the two should part ways.
She led Eric out of the bar, afraid to look back at the
girl who had shaken her so,
But Ashley had followed behind, stepping ever so
lightly so Donna could never have known.
Greeted outside by a calm, heavy snow, it was Ashley
who first took a murderous action.
The trash bag she took from inside was pulled over
poor Donna and then she was yanked in a fraction
Of a second to the ground where she landed face first;
what was worse than the pain was the fear and betrayal
She felt as they stuffed her down into the trunk of her
own husband's car and the fright was near fatal.

*They drove her far outside the city, hours down old country roads*
*And through the mountains; what the destination was she*
*couldn't know.*
*At last the car was made to stop at God knew where; the*
*afternoon*
*Cast shadows on the ground that promised that the day was*
*ending soon.*
*Donna heard the trunk unlock; the door popped open and she*
*kicked*
*With rage at her assailants, but the two were just a step too*
*quick.*

*Ashley grabbed a leg and pulled her out while Eric stripped her*
*coat*
*And held her arms behind her back while Ashley took her by the*
*throat.*

They dragged her off into the woods while she
struggled, still puzzled as to why she was being abused.
They both let her scream 'till her voice had gone out as
they carried her on through the cold without shoes.
There was no one around within miles to see the cruel
smiles that flashed as the two threw her down.
What followed was savage; they ravaged and beat on
the girl 'till she couldn't get up from the ground.
They sat her weak body against a bare tree and prepared
to leave, stranding her there in the woods.
Ashley bent over and gave her a kiss on the lips; she'd
have fought it if only she could.
With a wink and a smile she turned and joined Eric,
who didn't say anything about what he'd done.
Donna watched hope get buried in snow as she saw the
two fading with the cold, setting sun.

*Eyes still wide with shock and horror, Donna waited there to die*
*And wondered why it happened, but the weather wouldn't let her*
*cry.*
*Blood was freezing, hands were shaking, raking at her frosted*
*skin;*
*Donna knew she didn't have a chance but hated giving in.*
*Breathing in grew harder as the icy world began to spin;*
*Hopeless anger overtook her as she thought of Ashley's grin.*
*Everything inside her made her want to beat the cold and win,*
*But wanting finds no purchase in the court of Summer's heartless*
*twin.*

Too battered and broken to manage survival, she finally let her eyes rest and laid still.

She gave up her hope and her wishes, embraced what was coming, and Winter moved in for the kill.

Her body gave ground as the sun settled down; it still took some time for the process to end.

Her last living thought was of Eric and how she had lost him and how unfair it had been.

Death was in store and her breath was no more as she fell to the gray she was destined to find.

A few moments later, the cold that had made her so lonely was something she didn't much mind.

But something was wrong, for she still felt awake; she had taken for granted what fate had in store.

She opened her eyes and saw everything just as she left it—no changes, no less and no more.

*Getting up was now so easy, Donna's mind could find no answers*
*'Till she turned around and found herself still frozen, broken, hampered.*
*All the world around her bound her down to watch her cry and shake;*
*She had tried with all her might to fight the cold and stay awake.*
*All the mercy left the soul that now could see its own dead frame*
*And she was now a goddess, looking out upon her new domain.*
*She was something wild, something heartless that could not be tamed*
*And there would be no quarter, for the Winter hurts us all the same.*

The Goddess left her name with her frame by the tree and let all the new fury inside her find room.

She was made of the wind and the cold, pouring rain and she knew she'd use both 'till her mind was consumed
With the havoc she'd cause—no reason to pause while her killers were out there enjoying the heat
Of a fire; the liars were hiding from ire they'd earned—they killed in the snow so they'd reap
The new storm that was coming to ruin their comfort; she moved with the speed of a hurricane gale
To the place where the two had fled after the deed had been done (a small cabin down a long, narrow trail).
She swept to the window and found the two cozy and dozing in front of a warm, happy fire.
The Goddess was angry all over again; the scene absolutely had reeked with desire.

*The air grew colder, wind grew bolder, windows cracked from all the strain.*
*Doors flew open, leaving them exposed to gales and driving rain.*
*Cabinets clattered, all their peace was shattered as they felt the cold*
*That rushed inside to end one of the saddest stories ever told.*
*The lovers tried to close the doors and windows but they tried in vain;*
*Nothing helped, for they enraged the Goddess of the Wind and Rain.*
*Another few degrees were lost and they were getting frightened now*
*Because they knew, despite it all, that Justice found them out somehow.*

Eric and Ashley decided to run; they were numb in the hands and the cabin was going
To fall in a minute. The wind was too strong and they wanted to leave before it really was snowing.

They fought their way out to the brutal outdoors in the
night where the Goddess and weather were waiting
To make them both pay for their actions that day; she
would make every step that they took well worth
hating.
They knew they could feel someone watching, and
knew just as well that they'd never feel comfort again.
They cried out apologies, only to lose them in throats
that were parched and the roar of the wind.
At last they had reached the inside of the car and
decided to drive just as far as they could,
But the only road out was a treacherous gauntlet of
turns and steep drop-offs that ran by the woods.

*Once the car had hit the road, the Goddess unleashed all her fury;*
*Wipers just weren't fast enough to keep the road from being*
*blurry.*
*Frozen rain had made the way impossible to drive through safely.*
*Still they drove, insistent that they stay the course and try escaping*
*'Till they hit a patch of ice; they lost control and had to skid.*
*Eric tried to slow down and recover but he never did.*
*Ashley had to jump and hit the road and watched in utter fright*
*While Eric's car slid off the road and disappeared from Ashley's*
*sight.*

She heard the car crash, heard the glass crack and
shatter, but other than that there was nary a sound;
She knew in an instant that Eric was dead and she
wasted no time getting up from the ground.
She ran to the woods on feet that were numb; she was
coming to learn how foreign she felt
In the merciless cold where the comfort is gone—she
was coming to learn how sorry she felt.

She staggered through blackness and branches and rain,
insane with the fear that the Goddess instilled,
Until something tripped her and made her fall down in
the snow—the corpse of the girl she had killed.
She crawled to it quickly and begged for forgiveness,
crying through eyes that just couldn't make tears.
The frost covered figure just stayed where it was, giving
no sign that her end wasn't near.

*The Goddess saw her kneel and made her feel the pain that she
had felt;*
*She made it cold enough to freeze the girl exactly where she knelt.*
*All through life that beauty queen had thought of beauty as her
savior;*
*Someone should have told the girl that Winter doesn't grant us
favors.*
*All through life she found a way to cast away another's blame;*
*But there's no point in casting blame since Winter hurts us all the
same.*
*Still she's frozen in the forest, bowing to the one she wronged;*
*The air will get no warmer there until the Goddess moves along.*

www.ingramcontent.com/pod-product-compliance
Lightning Source LLC
Chambersburg PA
CBHW070525030426
42337CB00016B/2102